To Be Eaten By Mice

Robyn Mathison

To Be Eaten By Mice

To Be Eaten By Mice
ISBN 978 1 74027 558 3
Copyright © text Robyn Mathison 2009
Copyright © cover design Alexander Okenyo 2009

First published 2009
Reprinted 2016

Ginninderra Press
PO Box 3461 Port Adelaide SA 5015 Australia
www.ginninderrapress.com.au

Contents

Who's Counting?	7
Great-grandmother's Letter	8
therefore, ye soft pipes, play on	9
A Gift for Travel	10
Choosing Buttons	11
Ragged Blossom	13
Cinema With Mum	15
Country Hospital	16
Lost Boys	17
Mother sits with me…	19
The Matriarchs' Relay	20
Breakfast in Bed	21
Golden Years	22
A Monday Morning Thought	23
Morning Again	24
Wake-up Call	25
Dog	26
Watchdog	27
Bedside Sphinx	28
Sleeping with Cats	29
Pondus the Penguin Dreams of Home	30
Philomel	31
Dark Messengers	32
Heartfelt	33
Bushwalker	34
Bennett's Wallaby	35
Running Through the Stars	36
Aquilegia	37
Eucalyptus ficifolia	39
Liberating the Lemur	40
After discussing global warming	42
In the City Desert	43
Outsiders	44
Amelia?	45
In Adelaide	46

North-east Farmer	47
An Auspicious Marriage	49
The Clever Country	50
Yellow Roses	53
Whiter than White	54
Coda to the Sad Song	55
Hypochondria	56
Thicker than Water	57
Double Mastectomy	58
Marooned	59
Grief and Consolation	61
Reading Beowulf	62
Epistle	63
Republican Dreaming	64
Foreign Policy	65
My Sort of Technology	66
Haiku, Faux haiku & Tanka	67
Fledgling	69
Workshop	70
Day Job	71
My hens give advice on poetry	72
Quiet House	73
Fruit-bowl Moments	74
Mist	75
Sunday Solstice	76
Remembering Jeremiah Chapter Two	77
The Lesser Arts	78
Knitting's for the Birds	79
Secret Garden	80
Pot-pourri	81
Seasonal Eating	82
Wainewright Poem	83
To a Nightshade	84
The Would-be Percussionist	85
Tears for a Jazz Man	86
Desert Song Senryu	87
Acknowledgements	88

Who's Counting?

Over thirty years ago
my son proudly told me,
'Grandma says
our family has been here
for five generations.'

I recall old family stories
of great-grandparents
and their siblings,
Australian-born children
of pioneers from Ireland.

I wonder who
can do the calculations
now that we include
Aboriginal forebears
in the family tree.

Great-grandmother's Letter

Dear IVF Fairy,
I write to remind you
that once
you offered me three wishes.
It's time now to claim them.

For my hundredth birthday
I'd like you to bring me
a facelift,
a baby –
and what was the other one?

Oh yes, my telegram
from the Queen.

therefore, ye soft pipes, play on

My grandmother taught me
embroidery stitches,
crochet and knitting
and the names of flowers.
We spent a lot of our time
talking.

She was stone deaf
by the time she was thirty,
thirty years before I was born.
She always carried pencil and paper,
and though she could lip read,
I wrote and wrote long notes
to her.

Grandma's voice was loud
and clear. In St Thomas's
she always led the singing.
Once in the opening hymn
the organist dared to be different.
Halfway through the first verse
he faltered mid-phrase
and had to change his tune to hers.
Hers was traditional.

Although she lived
till I was well past twenty,
Grandma never heard me
speak or laugh or cry,
or sing.

A Gift for Travel

My mother cuts an apple into quarters.
I watch the deft way she nicks out
core and seeds. Crisp sounds
transport me and my hands mimic hers
as if I feel the smooth pearl handle
of the tiny fruit knife she gave me
when I first left home at nineteen.

Her gift is always with me,
its shiny silver blade sheathed
in leather now softened with wear.
It has served me well on all my travels –
cutting chunks of cheese,
slitting open letters,
tightening loose screws,
sharpening pencils –
and I couldn't count the apples
it has cut and quartered
over scores of years.

I breathe the scent of apple in my mother's kitchen
and for one sharp moment
it is as if
a ghostly whiff of coal smoke
wafts in the open window of a train.

Choosing Buttons

At the haby counter
of the shop in the main street,
perched on a high stool
I'd sit beside my mother
while Mr Bashir
brought out trays
of cards of buttons.

Mum would hold these
against scraps of fabric
or looped and twisted
skeins of wool,
sometimes going to the doorway
to check the colour in the daylight.
She had to find the perfect buttons
to set off or to match
whatever she was making.

There'd be big ones for a topcoat;
sixpence-sized or smaller
to fit knitted buttonholes
in the bands of my new cardies;
blue ones smaller than threepences
for the boys' new school shirts;
and for the yokes of matinee
jackets for my older cousins' babies
there'd be cards of tiny white ones,
lustrous mother of pearl.

At home when a button was lost
it was my favourite job
to search the button tin
to find the matching size and colour
of the missing one.
I loved the subdued button chatter
as my fingers stirred and sifted
and I scooped out rattling handfuls
on to the kitchen table
where I'd shift and sort them
into button families.
All the special odd ones
I'd keep aside to play with
while Mum did the mending.

What flowing cloak or mantle
had the big green one once fastened?
What Cinderella garment
was the clear glass one cut from?
Had an elf-smith worked the metal
for that precious little circle
of silver filigree?
Did gangs of gnomes
make all the white ones?
There were so many of these
of every size possible:
of cloth-covered metal
or rounds cut from pearl shell, narwhal tusk,
old yellowish bone.

Ragged Blossom

Wattlebirds and green parrots
have spent all this morning
upside down in the flowering
gum tree, feeding rowdily.
Shreds of pale pink blossom
litter the ground.

I remember going
to a fancy-dress frolic
dressed as Bib or Bub –
I can't remember now
which of the gumnut babies
I was meant to be.
I wore Grandpa's felt beret
as my gumnut cap,
a fitted green bodice
and a frothy pink tutu
that belled out and rustled dryly
around my knees.

Mum sewed my costume
on the faithful treadle Singer.
It wasn't made of cotton tulle:
because of wartime rationing
Mum used crepe paper, sheets
and sheets of pink, one of green.

The rest of that summer
I played Bib and Bub games
on the shady side verandah,
whispering to myself
tales of my escapes from snakes
and wicked banksia men.

I sobbed and sobbed when winter
came and my tattered finery
was tied into a bundle
with old *Argus*es and *Herald*s
for the war-effort paper bale
at the Post Office in town.

Cinema With Mum

for Michael and Jude

When all around us other children
crackled bags of popcorn and potato chips
or indulged in Jaffa-rolling in the aisles,
when we whispered, 'Mum, we're hungry!'
she'd rummage in the backpack
and produce crisp apples –
Gravensteins, Jonathons,
Golden Delicious, hybrid Jonagolds,
Pink Ladies, tart Grannies,
Geeveston Fannies, and once
a giant King Alfred to share.
The variety depended on
just when in apple season
we went to see a film.

Country Hospital

We visited each afternoon
that long, hot summer,
sat where plane-tree shade
sometimes made a breeze
on the wide verandah, where
at one end lay King Fan,
the old market gardener,
hawking and spitting,
dying of consumption,
but always returning
Mum's soft greeting.
My older brother's bed
was at the other end
but close enough to see
when King Fan needed
the nurse's attention
and he had to call her.

The doctor said my brother
had a glandular fever,
its cause unknown,
as was any treatment
other than bed rest.
You can't be too careful:
it might be contagious!
This light and airy place
that caught the morning
sunshine was a 1940s version
of an isolation ward.

Lost Boys

The ghosts of my dead brothers
were only laid to rest
the other day.
They were born
nine and seven years
before me, but died
before we children
who came later
could ever get to know them.

Two brothers and I
always thought ourselves
Mum's family of three.
Those other birthdays
were never celebrated,
as far as I remember,
and those boys we didn't know
were hardly ever mentioned,
yet were always there.

For sixty years
I pictured them
in school shorts and sandals
inhabiting some mythic place
with Peter Pan.
But last October
I realised
that Mum had gone on
counting all their years.

On the fifteenth she said to me,
'Today is Alan's
seventieth birthday,'
and two months later,
'Alexander is sixty-eight today.'

Now Mum has died
aged ninety-four
and memories of Alan,
born in 1929,
and Alexander, 1931,
have left this world with her.

Mother sits with me...

after Jack Gilbert

Mother sits with me in my room
holding the old cat in her arms.
We try to decide whether animals, too, feel grief.
I tell about the young ewe in the garden
bleating and bleating to her stillborn lamb
long after I'd taken the body away.
She says that's how it was for her
when her babies died
but she had to do her bleating silently.
I say, 'That's how I grieved for you.'
She says, 'Now you can cry.'
and hands me the cat.
We listen to her purring, purring.
Then mother fades and leaves me in my room.

The Matriarchs' Relay

This event's history is far older than Olympia.
Its track is wide, circling on forever.
The women with the torches run side by side,
not a bit competitive, yet
the running is fast, the going often hard.

Mum and Grandma are behind me
with all my aunts and great-aunts
and almost all my cousins.
They've all had their turn.

Along the track I see my daughter,
my son's wife, her daughter,
nieces and their children.
I can't see all their faces
but each head of bright hair
shines in the sun.

At first I flinch
from the heat of the flame.
I'm not ready and the torch is heavy
but I can't refuse it.
I grasp it tightly and looking ahead
to my red-haired granddaughter,
I take a deep breath
and slowly at first,
I begin to run.

Breakfast in Bed

For once my granddaughter
wakes before me.
As I surface from sleep
she hands me my notebook
and fountain pen.

'Good morning, Grandma.
You've just got time
to write one little poem
before you make our toast
and orange juice
and your pot of tea.'

She goes to the window sill
already gathering
beach pebbles, shells,
one perfect gull's feather
and a rose-quartz crystal.
'While you're writing
I'll decorate our tray.'

Golden Years

The telephone rings.
I agree to attend
a special meeting.
There goes this week's
one free day.
I run to fetch the washing in.
Looks as if I'll be walking
the dogs in the rain.
I must get bread and vegetables.
Do I need milk as well?
My granddaughter's coming.
If she gets straight to sleep
after tea and stories
I might just catch
that radio programme
and finish the book
that's due back tomorrow
and can't be extended.
I wonder what time
they're coming to get her
in the morning?
I mustn't forget
my doctor's appointment
or to send those birthday cards.
Make a list now.
There's too much happening,
not enough time.

Perhaps I can reach dynamic equilibrium
if I get a rocking chair.

A Monday Morning Thought

My life's
a piece of
rope the
dog's been
worrying.

I need
to gather
the long
frayed ends,
re-plait it.

Morning Again

I wake to lilting squeaks
and rasping squawks
of little wattlebirds,
chuckles and twitters
of noisy miners
feeding in white blossom
on the blue gum tree.

The grey geography of sky
becomes a mountain range of cloud
on a wash of palest blue.
Sunlight strikes a crystal
hanging in the open window,
paints gently bobbing rainbows
on the room's white walls.

Wake-up Call

Something nudges
gently at her shoulder,
wakes her from a dream.

Six inches
from her pillow
the grinning kelpie

pants warm dog breath
right into her nose.
It's the thick, rich brown

of packet gravy
and smells
of last night's bone.

Dog

My relationships with dogs
seem more successful
than with any lover.

Beau, Rastus, Rabbie,
Champ, King, Gypsy,
Tiger, Midnight, Piglet –

their total years with me
are one hundred and thirty-seven,
an average of fifteen (point two repeating).

Fifteen years!
That would be a dog's age
with men.

Watchdog

I am going through the wardrobe
trying things on,
culling clothes
I'll never wear again.
At the open window
the young kelpie, Maggie
stands stock still,
ears pricked, head cocked,
watching me.

I tie a long silk scarf
around my head
and its purple paisley pattern
swirls memories.
I raise my arms and hum
a Bob Dylan tune.
The soft green kaftan
I used to wear, when my long hair
was golden and my children were small,
wafts hints of incense –
sandalwood, patchouli –
as I dance a slow
barefoot circle.

Suddenly Maggie is dingo-eyed,
leaping at the window
barking, barking,
barking at the strange
intruder in my room.
She does not stop
until I take off the scarf
and softly speak her name.

Bedside Sphinx

Sunlight flickers
gold filigree,
bird calls criss-cross
the wild garden.
The clock tick ticks.
The enigmatic cat
stares fixedly.
She sits in a jumble
of pens and books
meditating
on the novel and poetry
or perhaps just watching
the second hand go round.
Now she blinks,
looks at me
with that half smile,
slit-eyed
with mystery.

Sleeping with Cats

They curl round
beside me
in the doona,
weighing it down
all round my body.
The bed's warm
as cats' breath,
my ears furred
with purring.
I drift into sleep
and they dream
their cat dreams
into me.

Pondus the Penguin Dreams of Home

It's a soft life in Copenhagen
with Jerry in keeper's cap and clogs
and daily buckets of herrings
and all those children in sturdy boots,
woolly caps and mittens.
How they laugh and clap
to see me follow Jerry,
flipper-feet splayed at ten-to-two
just like Charlie Chaplin's,
my fringed red scarf swinging.

When the zoo is shut and children have gone
the lion roars through the dark
for thornbush and golden Veld-grass;
monkeys scream for the steamy jungle.
I go then in sleep to the land's edge,
launch myself, a dark arrow,
to fly through the sea to a world of white,
packed snow and ice that's deeper than white,
that's pale, pale jade
and cold, hard, milky blue.

Pondus is the central character in a children's book, *Pondus the Penguin*, written and photographed by Ivar Myrhoj.

Philomel

Giacomo Leopardi
was in Europe, I believe,
when he wrote *In Praise of Birds*.
He would have studied blackbirds,
sparrows, starlings
and sweet-voiced nightingales.

Birds, he tells us,
though free and independent,
are none the less sensitive
to the presence of man.
Where people are gentler,
birdsong is, too.

A kookaburra laughs
and I ponder his theory
in this hemisphere.
Till 1788, I wonder,
was the singing of wattlebirds
honey-sweet?

Dark Messengers

If it's true that birds
are divine messengers
I wonder what it means
that ravens nested
in my blue gum tree last spring.

The young birds raised there,
noisy adolescents now,
gather at the nest site
first thing every morning,
strip bark, squawk and squabble.

'Ah ah aah,' another raven cries
from further down the hill.
They call in answer
and fly from my garden
on slow, creaking wings.

Heartfelt

As I walked up Criterion Street
a homing starling caught
in a sudden gust of wind
flew headlong into me,
crashed on my left breast.

The impact nearly felled me.
I staggered back in shock and pain.
Is a heart attack like this,
a kamikaze bird striking the chest
like a tiny plane?

The bird lay on the pavement
gape-beaked, panting, its gaze
one beady eye fixed on me.
'Don't die of shock,' I whispered.
It twitched its feet and fluttered

and next thing was flying
in the direction of Mathers Lane.
Good idea, I thought. She's going
to the Catholic Women's rest rooms
for a nice hot cup of tea.

Bushwalker

She eases off wet boots
and the pack from her shoulders.
The Trangia sings briefly
for hot black tea.
Cocooned in her sleeping bag
she listens to silence,
her little tent hidden
in mist-shrouded trees.

Bennett's Wallaby

Campsite visitor –
from a red enamel mug
she sips black tea.
She accepts my gift
of quartered green apple
with delicacy.

She settles then
at the edge of firelight,
chews contentedly.

Running Through the Stars

Is our old front paddock
sprinkled once again
with Early Nancy lilies,
Anguillaria dioica,
those harbingers of spring?

It's over sixty years
since I picked that first fistful
to give to my mother
and the blue glass eyebath
held those too-short stems.

Is that paddock even still there,
hiding its secret bulbs
of Blackman's Potatoes?
It might be under houses now:
the town has grown since then.

Perhaps now, in rooms there,
children wake, puzzled
by half-remembered dreams.
Through drifts of Golden Sun-moths
they've been running barefoot
in a paddock of Wallaby-grass,
rough pasture dotted
with tiny, white,
purple-hearted stars.

Aquilegia

for Meg

Your aunt Judi said,
'Look at all the bumblebees
in the grannies' bonnets.'

'Grandma calls those Aquilegia,'
you replied. 'When I was little
I called them fairy flowers.'

Soon other grannies' bonnets,
simply-stitched caps of plain calico,
will bloom in South Hobart

at the old Female Factory
where so many of our grannies
laboured as young girls.

There'll be one for Ellen Murphy
your four-times-great-grandmother
who came here at thirteen,

a pale-complexioned nursegirl
who was accused of stealing
four books and a fan.

She came to Van Diemen's Land
aboard the *America* in 1831
after spending time in Newgate.

She then served time
in all the female factories here
and in private homes.

At twenty-two she married
George Mainwaring, farmer
and former convict.

Between them they raised
eleven children before Ellen died
of stomach cancer, aged fifty-two.

Like the busy bumblebees
imported from New Zealand,
shiploads of convict women

were forcibly transported
from England, Scotland, Ireland,
and though at first reviled,

they stayed and colonised,
making their homes
all around Tasmania.

Their farms and cottage gardens
raised crops and crops of babies,
seas of fairy flowers.

Eucalyptus ficifolia

The red-flowering gum tree
died about four years ago
but still drops twigs and limb
wood for my fire.

Yellow wattlebirds
swing on the skeleton,
cavort and squawk and carry on
harsh conversations.

'Remember when
we used to come here
for the nectar? After rain
we'd shower in the leaves.'

I share their loss: shade
and nectared blossom.
It's OK, birds, I tell them,
I've planted another one.

It's here in the garden
too small yet to flower,
but it's coming on;
it's coming on.

Liberating the Lemur

for Deborah St Leger

The lemur is brought
from the museum dungeon
with pelts of animals,
a fierce-faced tiger
and stuffed exotic birds.
Caught by some forgotten
taxidermist's art,
it surveys passers-by
with glassy stare.
How many years has it held this pose,
dust gathering in once-glossy fur?

The artist captures the lemur
with deft strokes of ink
and watercolour,
rolls the drawing quickly
into a cylinder
and spirits it away.
It's the ninth of May,
first day of Lemuria,
ancient Roman Festival of the Dead.

The drawing unfurls.
Lemur dreams of forests
on a lost continent
deep beneath the Indian Ocean.
Moonlight falls
on a pale pointy face,
glints in round dark eyes.

Suddenly lithe and agile,
with a flaunt of upturned
tail and just a hint of smile,
Lemur skitters into the night
and heads for Madagascar.
In the empty studio
rice paper rustles a breath
of vanilla-scented air.

After discussing global warming

I dream I'm Mrs Noah
sitting snugly in the ark
as the floodwaters rise.
I've been darning Noah's socks
but I put the work basket
and wooden mushroom aside.
Who ever would have thought
I would become grandmother
to this boatload of creatures?

The giraffes' new baby
stands splay-legged
by my gently rocking chair.
I love his long eyelashes,
his camel-like half smile
and, under my hand,
the silky smoothness
and warm tessellated patches
of his shiny supple hide.

In the City Desert

1.

Raven's at the top
of *Eucalyptus globulus*
calling up the weather.

Ah ah aah…
we have scudding cloud
on a pale sunny sky.

Ah ah aah…
petals of plum blossom
blow on the wind.

2.

In a street of car yards
and commercial premises
opposite the Royal

Automobile Club of Tasmania
above the roar
of Friday rush-hour traffic

on the roof
of Computer Technical Services
a flirt of tail feathers

balances beak-dipping.
Raven's on the water tank
drinking.

Outsiders

He slouches on the bench
outside the real estate agency
watching the world go by.

I hear a passing woman say,
'He's got mental illness
written all over him.'

No expression
crosses his face.
He looks through the woman

and her friend, stopped
at the pedestrian crossing.
When the lights change

he springs up, retrieves
a tissue they have dropped
and, holding it delicately

by one corner,
drops it, with a flourish,
into the bin.

On his way back to his vantage point
he catches my eye
and grins.

Amelia?

She was a little woman,
white-haired, in sensible shoes,
tweed skirt and twinset:
somebody's grandma.
Late afternoon light
gave her a halo.
I felt we'd smile and say hello
as we passed each other.

Just as the lights changed
she raised her arms up and out
like a kindergarten child
who is pretending
she's a little aeroplane.
I stepped off the kerb
and found myself looking up at the sky
above the intersection.

A seagull banked and wheeled
and flew off towards the mountain.
No one came towards me.
There was no sign of her.

In Adelaide

Flowering shrubs and roses
line up along the fences,
bright annuals crowd
at the edges of the lawns.
Across the narrow roadway
houses exchange glances
from behind lace curtains,
or peek obliquely
through Venetian blinds.

At six o'clock each morning
a woman in a tracksuit
and silent sneakers
walks briskly down the street
not looking towards the windows.
Even I can tell
she's not a resident.
She's pulled by a large
Alsatian on a string.

In the late afternoons
doves and top-knot pigeons
cease their plaintive calling
from leafy street trees
and ever so decorously
stroll along the footpaths.
Like old-fashioned nuns
or latter-day Mormons
they are always in pairs.

North-east Farmer

i.m. Sandy Rosier

1. Weather

I hate this wind.
We never had wind like this
when I was a young feller.
Of course there was wind then
but the trees absorbed it–
and we always had enough rain.
But they've cut the trees down,
cut them all down,
and now we've got this wind.

2. Mt Victoria

I can take you to the old mine
on Mt Victoria. I reckon
there's still lots of gold in there
and if it's true that the tigers
haven't died out
I reckon they're up there as well.
I worked up there
when I was a young bloke
before I had the farm.

I can show you the place
where I lost my team,
where my bullock team
went over the side
just near the cyanide dam.
I was lucky they didn't fall in.

There's eagles' nests up there too,
wedge-tailed eagles.
I can show you those as well.
We'll go in the morning,
tomorrow morning
as soon as the milking's done.

3. Sheep

I've got a fair few of these
little sheep, these little Polwarths.
They're much smaller
than the Romneys
or the big Border Leicesters
that the shearers don't like
handling. If I can't
sell the wool this year
I can sell the Polwarths.

I can tie a ribbon
round their necks
with a little silver bell
and sell them in town
for people's gardens.
I can put a sign up
down on the road
just by the driveway:
Garden Sheep for Sale.

An Auspicious Marriage

A wind-filled garbage bag
is a magic orange cushion
swooping towards the sea.
A cruise-ship funnel,
air-sea-rescue orange,
bisects river/sky.
An orange bath mat flaps
on a neighbour's washing line.

I become obsessed
with a colour combination,
place eight ripe apricots
in a sky-blue Chinese bowl.
Then I read Alexander Theroux:
Orange is the wife of blue.

Alexander Theroux: *The Secondary Colours: Three Essays* [Henry Holt, New York 1996]

The Clever Country

In nineteen fifty-nine
at John Martin's summer sale,
I bought a pair of straight-legged
rather tight black jeans.
'You're not a widgie, are you?'
my mother asked,
still trying to accept
that despite his education
the fellow I'd just married
followed horse racing
and even attended the trots
at Wayville Showground.

There he would meet
my friend Laszlo,
gentle philosopher,
incurable optimist,
a soft-voiced Hungarian
over twenty years our senior.
I had first met Laszlo
in nineteen fifty-seven
when he and I attended
the same lectures
and tutorials
at the university.

He had introduced me
to a new rich world
of European
thought and culture,
beyond the narrow bounds
of the country and empire
that was all I knew.
He'd already served time here –
two years on the railway
between Perth and Adelaide –
before he was permitted
to return to university.

There he repeated
his studies all over again
only to be told that
because of halting English,
there could never be
academic employment
in this country for him.

He knew he could go back
to work on the railway,
perhaps on a suburban line,
but instead decided to become
a professional punter.

In those far-off days
my young husband was no philosopher.
The only thing he and Laszlo had in common,
apart from optimism,
was their devotion to systems
they were sure one day would win.
Perhaps they should
have listened to my mother,
for time has shown
that neither man was destined
to make a fortune, or a living
in a racecourse betting ring.

Yellow Roses

You arrive on my doorstep
years later
with yellow roses.
'My ex-lovers,' you say,
'are always my friends.'

I remember nights of lust
and silence.
You were my lover.
Soft petals fall.
You were never my friend.

Whiter than White

I answer the telephone
at my friend's house.
It's her former husband
wanting one of their children.

Got any washing out?
he asks conversationally.
You might want to get it in.
There's rain blowing up

quite fast along the river.
Mind you, when it rains
I leave mine out.
I've found a good rinse

with rainwater
and then a day of sun
always brings the whites up
ever so much whiter.

Coda to the Sad Song

In nineteen seventy
I pawned my wedding
and engagement rings
to buy my daughter shoes.
I never did get them
out of hock again.

But time's a great redeemer.
Little feet grow, fingers thicken,
girls grow into women,
old sadness disappears.
So let the lamenting fiddle
break into jigs and reels.

Hypochondria

Please don't tell me
about your hypertension
or your hernia
or your great-aunt Nell's
circulation problem.

I've got enough trouble
watching for subtle
metabolic changes,
wondering if they're important,
what they mean.

Is my heartbeat normal?
Have I got a fever?
Am I just thirsty,
or is this a signal
of late-onset
diabetes?

Please don't even mention
any sort of illness –
yours or anyone's –
or I'll be manifesting
all the symptoms
within the hour.

Thicker than Water

My brother's letter tells me
I should have myself tested
and alert my children, especially
my son, to the probability
that I have Genetic Haemochromatosis.

He has just been diagnosed
with this blood disorder.
His DNA tests suggest
that both of our late parents
must have carried the rogue genes.

He writes, 'It means the body
produces too much iron
and lays this burden down
in the vital organs, especially
heart and liver. Eventually it kills you.'

I listen to the beat of the little red engine,
my faithful heart pumping, pumping,
shunting its heavy freight around
the underground railway of arteries and veins.
All this time is my body slowly rusting?

Double Mastectomy

After the surgery
she touches herself shyly
the way he might
if he ever touches her again.

She remembers reading
amputees feel aches and itches
in phantom limbs,
thinks about the memories

her body holds, wonders
if, when she hears a baby cry,
she'll feel lost nipples prick
with engorgement's almost-pain

and then the sweet release
as the milk lets down.

Marooned

For weeks she had lain there
being turned at intervals,
rolled aside and back again
as they washed her body
and for dressings, clothes
and bedding to be changed.

Then came sitting
out of bed in a chair,
first tentative steps
across the ward,
steadied and supported
by strong young arms.

She walked then, unaided,
as far as the island
of the nurse's station
and slowly back again
to her curtained corner
of that windowless room.

One day her slippered feet
hobbled to the daylight
at the corridor's end.
She looked out the window,
made out the contours
of a distant line of hills.

Beyond these, she knew
sky met ocean.
She closed her eyes,
saw herself standing
beside piled driftwood
in the white dunes.

She heard the wash of waves
and a gull's plaintive cry.
She would wait now,
matches ready
to light the beacon
the instant a ship appeared.

Grief and Consolation

In these dark days of winter
too many friends are leaving.
Three younger women,
reinventing themselves,
go to build new lives
far from this island's shores.
They will write to me.
Only silence will mark the one
who is scattered ash now,
the other, buried in the ground.

In my dream, the small grey car
leaves rain-washed city streets,
follows a winding road through scrub
and under dripping trees.
I'm behind the wheel
driving confidently,
for I know that where I'm heading
tomorrow's sun will dry my tears.

Reading Beowulf

'Grendel is evil personified,'
the teacher tells me.

I can't help thinking
of Grendel's mother:

she's just as terrible
as the monstrous Grendel.

What sort of childhood
did Grendel have

with this vengeful woman?
Is she the mother of all evil?

Is this old saga still our story
in two thousand and three AD?

Are we caught forever
between warring forces

of Good and Evil, doomed
to dwell in no-man's land,

one day singing in the meadhouse,
next day cowering in the bothies?

Is Peace possible
in this world?

Epistle

Dear Barbara Thiering,
I am writing to thank you
for all your work proving
what I, and many a woman before me,
have long suspected.

Mind you, they won't like it,
the men – you saying that
Jesus was only
an ordinary man, albeit Essene
and sensitive with it.
No, they won't like it at all.

They're frightened of us.
They ridicule crones,
wise older women.
Remember the witches?
Men hunted us down
all over Europe,
the flames of the bone-fires
feeding their fear.

And don't think
this new age of men
will prove to be any more humane.
Two thousand years
is a long-term investment.
Christendom's smaller,
interest is falling:
More is at stake
for those churchmen left
in the world today.

Republican Dreaming

For Mary Bamblett

In afternoon heat I'm under the pepper tree
tidying the bowerbird cubby house.
I neaten twig walls, whisk floors with a needle-broom
picked this morning from the playground pine tree.
I rearrange goblets of coloured bottle glass,
set out the tea set of precious shards.

Then you come, peering through trailing curtains –
feathery leaves, pink peppercorns.
I look up, smile, move a teacup.
'Say you're a visitor,' I say.
'Say I'm the Queen,' you answer;
'I've come to visit you from England.'

I sit back on dusty haunches,
take off my invisible apron,
hold back pepper-tree branches in welcome.
'Come in, Your Royal Highness.
I've just made a pot of tea.'

Foreign Policy

East Timorese refugees waited fourteen years
for Australia to recognise
they were not Portuguese.

How long will it take now
for Australian people like you,
like me, to convince the world
we are human beings?

My Sort of Technology

How I need it: a remote
control mechanism
to switch off
at the press of a button
not just the radio or TV
but the politician himself,
silencing mealy-mouthed
obfuscations
and bare-faced lies.

Haiku, Faux haiku & Tanka

above the ocean
night birds fly
shadows on the moon

bare trees net birds on mackerel sky

cats in the garden
in the pansy patch
kitten flowers

darting bright glances
bold sparrows peck spilt sugar
from café tables
I bask in winter sunshine
as my cup of coffee cools

dawn light on water
my dead mother comes to me
a silver gull

dry earth waits for rain
beneath indigo storm clouds
seabirds fly inland
as the first fat raindrops fall
I dash to fetch washing in

flights of pigeons
winged messengers
letters from friends

leaf fall gives the mountain back to me

night wind
in the jasmine
scented stars fall

November brings
jasmine and honeysuckle
my birthday too

patchwork
scraps of cloth
memories

Fledgling

My little sparrow poem
curls claws
close around the platen.
'Come on,' I coax.
'It's time to leave
the typewriter
and fly into the world.
You'll meet editors,
perhaps even
a publisher and readers.'

The critic on my shoulder stirs.
Raven strops her beak.
Shadows of great wings
darken the room.

Workshop

Ten women write –
the sound of pens on paper
silkworms in a shoebox
munching mulberry leaves.

How long will it be
before whispering words
settle into silence
spinning their cocoons?

How much longer still
until they chew
through golden silk
to emerge as white-moth poems?

Day Job

I'm sitting at my desk
working on a poem
when the phone rings
insistently.
It's a neighbour.
Her baby is asleep
just when she needs
to keep an appointment
with her doctor.
Can I babysit, please,
just for an hour or so?

Three hours later
she returns, red-faced,
on the verge of tears,
apologising most profusely.
Meanwhile I have changed
the baby, fed him,
sung songs,
played peek-a-boo,
discovered he has dimples
when he smiles
and crows with laughter.

I remember what someone else said,
whose name I've forgotten:
'I don't live to work.
I live to live,' and realise
the poem will keep
for another day.

My hens give advice on poetry

The world is full of cruelty and beauty:
a full moon rising gold above the river,
star travel through the cold night sky,
frost on grass blade and chook claw,
leaves winking in wing-stretch morning sun.

Take your poems out into the garden,
think and speak them, try to hum them.
Pick some seed heads, dig some mulch in,
nip back a tendril of rampant creeper.
Stop and think your poems through again.

Your poems should strike the heart
with terror and with beauty.
As you settle down to write them
stop and ask yourself: Are they
fox-coloured? Do they sing?

Quiet House

How could you leave a house
where blue wrens and bandicoots
come to a scattering of oat flakes
on a sunny doorstep?

You have taken it, inside you
with herb garden, honey bees;
but images from visits there
live inside me.

I share a patch of sun
with yellow dog and red hen
side by side, sleeping
while I sit writing.

Where will memory be
when my body leaves?

Fruit-bowl Moments

withered kiwi fruit
under apples and lemons
little brown mouse body

cut passionfruit
weeps black-mascara tears
while violins sing

this grey-sky morning
a fat lemon promises
the sharp sting of sun

Mist

and mellow fruitfulness has come to my garden before mid-February
with new season's apples ripe on the tree and in the hedge there are
fat blackberries among thorns and blossom and rain-jewelled leaves.
I wake this morning to the liquid notes of grey butcherbirds' songs,
the darting calls of little wattlebirds and soft grey cloud shrouding trees.

Sunday Solstice

Mist clings in treetops
stirred only for moments
by flitting birds.

Sunlight fingers
the white room.
The year turns.

I pull on a sweater,
switch on the radio,
take up my pen.

Someone plays Mozart.
Piano notes scatter,
flick leaf shadows, sunbeams,

and Trinity Hill
peals a descant
of bells.

Remembering Jeremiah Chapter Two

Verse 25: Withhold thy foot from being unshod…

On summer Sunday mornings
my friend Helen's father
walks barefoot to the shops,
half a mile or more,
to buy the milk and paper.
With his dry hair all tousled
and wearing striped pyjamas,
he stops to talk to neighbours
out early picking roses
or pushing ticking mowers
over neat green lawns.

If I were Helen
I'd die of embarrassment.
On the 8.15 train on Monday morning
I pretend not to see him
reading the paper
in white shirt and business suit
and polished shoes.
From behind my Latin book
I peep at his ankles.
Dark wool hugs pale flesh,
blue veins, sharp angles of bones.

The Lesser Arts

'Have nothing in your houses that you do not know to be useful or believe to be beautiful.' – William Morris 1882

My mind's eye fills with flowers, books,
Turkish rugs on polished floorboards,
lean chairs soft with flowered cushions:
spare treasures tastefully arranged
as in *English House and Garden*.

I look around me, see my desk
piled with drafts, unanswered letters,
the kitchen full of last night's dishes,
tattered rugs, cats and dogs,
a mustard pot of dusty feathers.

No Red House or Kelmscott this,
but Anti-Scrape in extremis.
And I, not young *in dainty raiment*,
didn't catch the *News From Nowhere*
but watched *Time* steal *The Commonweal*.

Ah William, my youth's guide and mentor,
(*Socialism…Art and Labour…*)
your stem edict would preclude now
most things from my shabby house –
alas, including me.

Knitting's for the Birds

Mrs Plumpster knits and knits
a woollen jersey
as much like feathers
as knitting can be
and Borka
the featherless goose,
safe in Kew Gardens since 1963,
is just as she was
when my children knew her.
Now their children
share her story with me.

Like Mrs Plumpster
I still knit and knit.
Soft grey wool
stitches family
and tiny
multicoloured sweaters
save fairy penguins
after oil spills at sea.

Secret Garden

I step through an archway
of scrambling banksia roses
in full creamy bloom,
follow the well-worn brick path
bisecting a petal-strewn lawn.
I walk through the heart –
a four-chambered knot-garden
hedged with clipped lavender.
White roses lift open faces
to the gentle kiss of sun.
Over an old stone bench
now in deep green shade
pink roses spill from a wall.

A silent movement of air
wafts a dry scent I recognise.
A pot-pourri of roses,
lavender, grass, sunshine,
conjures soft cheeks
velvet-dusted with face powder.
As I breathe in scented air
beloved, long-dead women
are in that garden with me.

Pot-pourri

Dried rose petals
crumble
between my fingers.

Dark red perfume
permeates
the air,

evokes memory
of old love –
sweet, secure.

Seasonal Eating

1. Menu

Starter
Zucchini Soup
sefved with zucchini-bread croutons
and shaved Parmesan.

Main Course
Zucchini Frittata
served with zucchini & tomato salsa
and salad of grated zucchini & rocket leaves.

Dessert
Zucchini Cake
served with raspberry & zucchini coulis
and King Island cream.

2. Recipes

Apply direct to author
(please enclose ssae)
– or invent your own.

Wainewright Poem

for Julian Halls

avocado and apples
lemons
cheese
pine nuts and basil
garlic
couscous and lentils
Kalamata olives
coffee beans
bottle of red
mesclun salad leaves
Geoff Dyer painting
silk tie (with camels)
check St Vinnies (orange Penguins)
something quick for tea

To a Nightshade

after John Keats

Sundried tomato, I do sing to thee
a song of praise for sharpness and for red!
Each day I love to have you for my tea
in salad, or with pasta or on bread;
and with your cousin, plump dark aubergine –
another special favourite of mine –
you're so delicious added to a stew
and served with couscous and a glass of wine
accompanied by salad crisp and green
with oil and lemon dressing. Oh a queen
who wants a feast should make a meal of you!

The Would-be Percussionist

Humpty Dumpty
sits on the wall
contemplating the triangle.

His imagination strikes
suspended metal
in symphonic punctuation:

ting-a-ling-a-ling
and three bars on
a rolled metallic trill.

Limbless, he dreams.
Music of the spheres echoes
inside his fragile shell.

Tears for a Jazz Man

I am listening
to *Australian Classic Jazz Duets*.
Ian Pearce is on piano
and a haunting cornet sings
Wasting My Love on You.
A saxophone croons *San*;
the cornet wails
Blues Enough for Two
and *I'm in the Mood for Love*.
Long before the alto sax
plays *Cherry*, I am weeping
for the late, great Tom Baker,
remembering those giant hands
cradling reeds, cornet,
trombone, trumpet –
coaxing sweetness
from cornflakes-packet toys.

Desert Song Senryu

Music pulls fingers,
turns thighs, hips and shoulders in
belly-dance warm-up.

The clarinet's voice
breathes out bloodbeat and footfall
the dance has begun

We dance the echoes:
blind feet must follow, follow
the beat of the drum.

Acknowledgements

Some of the poems in this collection have been previously published:

A Gift for Travel, *RePUBlic Readings*; A Monday Morning Thought, *Versions Two* (Versions Press); After discussing global warming, *The Mozzie*; Amelia?, *Famous Reporter*; An Auspicious Marriage, *broad seat*; Bedside Sphinx, *The Mozzie*; Breakfast in Bed, *The Mozzie*; Bushwalker, *Micropress Oz*; Choosing Buttons, endangereddrawingtheline.com; Cinema with Mum, *The Poets' Republic*; Coda to the Sad Song, *Famous Reporter*; Country Hospital, *Running Through the Stars* (FAW Tas); Dark Messengers, *Poetry Matters*; Day Job, *Stylus*; Desert Song Senryu, *Famous Reporter*; Dog, *RePUBlic readings*; Double Mastectomy, *Poetrix*; Epistle, *Womanspeak*; Eucalyptus ficifolia, *Moorilla Mosaic* (Bumblebee Books); Fledgling, *The Poets' Republic*; Foreign Policy, *Stylus*; Fruit-bowl Moments, *The Poets' Republic*; Golden Years, *Stylus*; Great-grandmother's Letter, *Poetrix*; Grief and Consolation, *The Poets' Republic*; Haiku, Faux Haiku & Tanka, *Hobo, Famous Reporter, Centoria, Yellow Moon*; Heartfelt, *Famous Reporter*; Hypochondria, *RePUBlic readings*; In Adelaide, *Moorilla Mosaic*; In the City Desert, *Hobo*; Knitting's for the Birds, *From the Anabranch* (Poets Union); The Lesser Arts, *Resurgence* (UK); Liberating the Lemur, *Poetry Matters*; Lost Boys, *Bone of My Bone* (H. Annand); The Matriarchs' Relay, *The Mozzie*; Mist, *Poetry Matters*; North-east Farmer, *The Poets' Republic*; Outsiders, *The Mozzie*; Philomel, *Philomel & Wattlebird* (FAW Tas); Pondus the Penguin Dreams of Home, *Island*; Pot Pourri, *broad seat*; Quiet House, *Centoria*; Reading Beowulf, *The Mozzie*; Remembering Jeremiah Chapter Two, *RePUBlic Readings*; Republican Dreaming, *Redoubt*; Running Through the Stars, *Famous Reporter*; Seasonal Eating, *The Mozzie*; Secret Garden, *Island Reflections* (SWW Tasmania); Sleeping with Cats, *Marmalade's Book of Cats* (Marmalade); Sunday Solstice, *Moorilla Mosaic*; Therefore, ye soft pipes, play on, *Redoubt*; Wainewright Poem, *RePUBlic Readings*; Wake-up Call, *The Weekend Australian Review*; Watchdog, *Dogs of Our Lives* (Gloria B. Yates); Workshop, *Island*; The Would-be Percussionist, *Poetry Matters*; Yellow Roses, *Hobo*

www.ingramcontent.com/pod-product-compliance
Lightning Source LLC
Chambersburg PA
CBHW062142100526
44589CB00014B/1662